GALVESTON BAY

by M. Weber

CHERRY LAKE PUBLISHING • ANN ARBOR, MICHIGAN

Published in the United States of America by:

CHERRY LAKE PRESS

2395 South Huron Parkway, Suite 200, Ann Arbor, MI 48104
www.cherrylakepublishing.com

Reading Adviser: Marla Conn MS, Ed., Literacy specialist, Read-Ability, Inc.

Series Adviser: Amy Reese, Coordinator of Elementary Science; Howard County School System, MD; President of Maryland Science Supervisors Association

Book Design: Book Buddy Media

Photo Credits: ©Mai Vu/Getty Images, background (pattern), ©giocalde/Getty Images, cover (bottom left), ©iStockphoto/Getty Images, cover (lined paper), ©Trong Nguyen/Shutterstock, cover (front top), ©Rainer Lesniewski/Getty Images, cover (map), ©Pixabay, cover (red circle), ©Muangsatun/Shutterstock, cover (bottom right), ©Dollar Travelers/Shutterstock, 1, ©Sam Greenwood/Staff/Getty Images, 3 (bottom left), ©Riorita/Getty Images, 3 (bottom right), ©Nicole Stutterheim/EyeEm/Getty Images, 4, ©PeterHermesFurian/Getty Images, 6, ©Alan Vernon/Getty Images, 7, ©Crystal Eye Studio/Shutterstock, 8, ©United States Geolicial Survey/Wikimedia, 9, ©ultramarinfoto/Getty Images, 10 , ©Jim Dyson/Staff/Getty Images, 11, ©Natalia Kuzmina/Shutterstock, 13, ©Damocean/Getty Images, 14, ©Alisha Newton/Shutterstock, 15 (top), ©PETERLAKOMY/Getty Images, 16, ©gpflman/Getty Images, 17, ©KPG_Payless/Shutterstock, 18, ©Socha/Getty Images, 19, ©chitsanupong Pakdeekul/Shutterstock, 20, ©VitalisG/Getty Images, 21 (top), ©JeffCaughey/Getty Images, 21 (bottom), ©Tim Leviston/EyeEm/Getty Images, 22, ©Thomas Shea/Stringer/Getty Images, 23, ©Klaus Vedfelt/Getty Images, 24, ©Art Wager/Getty Images, 25, ©Monty Rakusen/Getty Images, 26, ©RoschetzkyIstockPhoto/Getty Images, 27, ©anna1311/Getty Images, 28 (water pitcher), ©nortongo/Getty Images, 28 (bowl), ©iStockphoto/Getty Images, 28 (food color), ©Rajni Singh / EyeEm/Getty Images, cover (back), ©Devanath/Pixabay, (paperclips), ©louanapires/Pixabay, (paper texture)

Library of Congress Cataloging-in-Publication Data has been filed and is available at catalog.loc.gov

Cherry Lake Publishing would like to acknowledge the work of the Partnership for 21st Century Learning, a Network of Battelle for Kids. Please visit *http://www.battelleforkids.org/networks/p21* for more information.

Printed in the United States of America
Corporate Graphics

CHERRY LAKE PRESS

CONTENTS

CHAPTER 1
The Systems of Galveston Bay 4

CHAPTER 2
The Galveston Bay Watershed...................8

CHAPTER 3
Plants and Animals of
Galveston Bay 12

CHAPTER 4
Impact on Plants from Estuaries
and Tributaries...18

CHAPTER 5
Humans and the Bay................................22

Activity.......................................28
Glossary 30
For More Information 31
Index 32

The Systems of Galveston Bay

Galveston Bay is located in Texas. It is on the coast of the Gulf of Mexico. Galveston Bay was named by a Spanish military leader in 1875. It is near the city of Houston. Galveston Bay is 35 miles (56 kilometers) long. It is 19 miles (30 km) wide. The bay is only about 7 feet (2 meters) deep on average. This makes it a very shallow bay. Galveston Bay is an **estuary**. An estuary is a type of bay where a freshwater river meets the ocean. In an estuary, the wide opening to the sea is freely connected to rivers.

Two rivers flow into Galveston Bay. The San Jacinto River and the Trinity River meet to bring freshwater to the Gulf of Mexico. The San Jacinto River also gives the city of Houston access to the ocean. It is the seventh-largest estuary in the United States.

Galveston Bay is an **ecosystem**. There are four important spheres of Earth systems. The **geosphere** is made up of the earth. This includes soil and land. The geosphere also includes the shape of the land. Glaciers melted at the end of the last Ice Age. This created the shorelines of Galveston Bay. Today the soil in Galveston Bay contain toxins. Toxins come from **pollution**. They can also come from events like oil spills.

Wetlands found in Galveston Bay mark the change between land and water.

All of the water around Galveston Bay makes up its **hydrosphere**. This includes both freshwater from rivers and saltwater from the ocean. All the water mixes together in the estuary. The hydrosphere also includes rainwater. It rains about 40 inches (102 centimeters) a year in Galveston. Water temperatures change depending on the season. In the winter, water temperature can be as low as 54 degrees Fahrenheit (12 degrees Celsius). It can be as high as 86°F (30°C) in hot summer months.

The **atmosphere** of Galveston Bay is made up of the layers of air surrounding the bay. Air temperatures are like water temperatures. The temperatures vary from season to season. The weather is mild. The average high in the winter is 60 to 70°F (16 to 21°C). During the summer, the air temperature is between 70 and 89°F (21 and 32°C). The climate is **humid**. There is also pollution in the air. Most of the air pollution comes from cities like Houston. This can affect the health of the bay.

* Brown pelicans stand on their eggs to keep them warm before the eggs hatch.

The wildlife in Galveston Bay is part of the **biosphere**. The biosphere also includes all plant life. Galveston Bay is home to many kinds of plants and animals. Freshwater brings in nutrients to the bay. Animals such as the brown pelican are common in Galveston Bay. They eat fish that live in the bay. The fish eat plants living in the water. Together they create a complete food chain.

CHAPTER 2

The Galveston Bay Watershed

A watershed is made up of connected bodies of water. The watershed of Galveston Bay is about 24,000 square miles (62,160 square km). It is a very large area. Half the population of Texas lives in the watershed area for Galveston Bay. The Galveston Bay watershed includes the Trinity River and San Jacinto River. It also includes the **tributaries** that flow into the rivers. The land and water around a river is called a river basin.

Watershed Diagram

The Galveston Bay watershed is a large estuary. Many rivers flow together. They meet in the Gulf of Mexico.

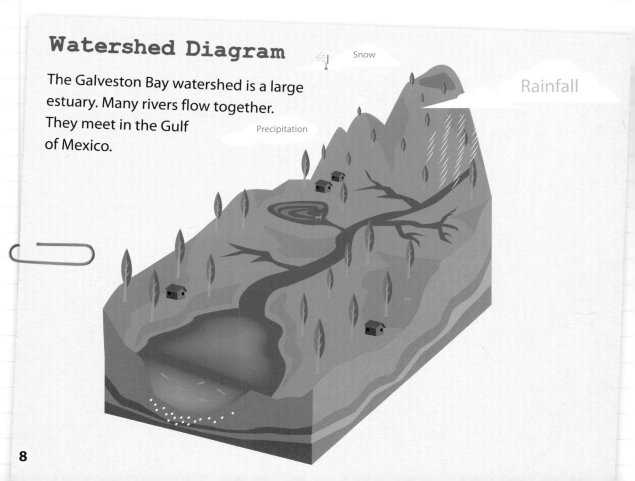

Snow

Rainfall

Precipitation

Water from Houston drains into Galveston Bay. The city tries to keep the water as clean as possible to keep the bay healthy.

Small bays are also part of Galveston Bay. East Bay, West Bay, and Trinity Bay are all smaller bays that connect to Galveston Bay. Areas called bayous are part of the bay. A bayou is a small area at the opening of a lake or river. Bayous are marshes. A marsh is a type of wetland. Many plants grow in marshes. During rainy seasons, bayous can flood.

There are three main types of **habitats** in the Galveston Bay watershed. Wetlands, sea grass meadows, and oyster reefs are all important to the bay. Wetlands can be found on the edges of the land. Estuarine wetlands are near the ocean. They contain both freshwater and saltwater. Estuarine wetlands change with the tides. Tides are the movement of the ocean. Freshwater wetlands are found far away from the ocean shore. They are part of a river or lake.

Sea grass meadows are named for the underwater plants that grow there. They look like underwater fields. The sea grass meadows are shallow. The water is very clear. It is also very salty. Between 1950 and 1980, about 1,700 acres (688 hectares) of sea grass meadow disappeared. They were hurt by human activity such as boating. Today people are working to **restore** the lost sea grass meadow.

* An area of sea grass the size of a soccer field can absorb pollution from driving a car 7,500 miles (12,070 km).

Oyster reefs are where oysters can be found in Galveston Bay. The reefs are in the open bay. Oyster reefs can be harmed when people take too many. Oyster shells can be used as a construction material. Oyster reefs can also be harmed in **hurricanes**.

The Galveston Bay watershed is important to the health of Texas. Estuaries provide water for human use. Estuaries like Galveston Bay are also important for **converting** carbon dioxide in the air. Too much carbon dioxide can be unhealthy. But Galveston Bay can convert carbon dioxide into oxygen like rainforests do. This keeps all people, animals, and plants healthy.

Christmas Bay

Christmas Bay Coastal Preserve is a special place. It is a small bay in the Galveston Bay estuary. It has never been used for commercial purposes. It is home to more kinds of fish than anywhere else in the bay. It is about 5,700 acres (2,307 ha). It is a guide for how a healthy bay should look.

CHAPTER 3

Plants and Animals of Galveston Bay

Estuaries like Galveston Bay are called the "nurseries of the seas." This is because they are so important to the life of plants and animals. Animals who live in the sea use the bay for food and safety. Plants and animals live in wetlands, sea grass meadows, and oyster reefs.

* Great blue herons are usually 3 to 4.5 feet (1 to 1.4 m) tall.

Wetlands are home to many types of wildlife. Almost all of the fish that live in the bay depend on wetlands. Even if they live in the sea, fish will often lay eggs in wetland areas. Wetlands are also important to white and brown shrimp. People aren't the only ones who like shrimp. Birds also eat them. Great blue herons use wetlands as feeding areas. Crabs live in the wetlands as well. When pollution runs into wetlands, it can contaminate the soil. Wetlands can sometimes help filter this pollution from reaching the ocean.

In the sea grass meadows, there is life beneath the surface of the water. Underwater grasses grow in shallow water. The water has to be shallow so sunlight can reach the grasses. Young shellfish grow up in the sea grass meadows. Some fish also lay eggs in the sea grass meadows. Today the sea grass meadows are threatened by human activity and climate change. The rising sea level has changed the depth of the sea grass meadows. This can make it hard for plants to grow.

All wildlife in Galveston Bay depend on each other for survival, including fish and sea grass.

On average, an oyster can filter about 2 gallons (7.6 l) of water per hour.

Oyster reefs are named for the animals that live there. Large clusters of oysters live together on the reefs. These clusters help to support other kinds of life too. Mollusks and crabs also live near the oyster reefs. Algae grows on oyster shells. The smaller animals bring bigger animals to the oyster reefs. Blue crabs like to eat oysters. When tides are low, birds will also eat oysters.

* The largest oyster in the world is 14 inches (36 cm) long.

Since 2003, the population of birds in Galveston Bay has been steady. Birds depend on a healthy bay. Some birds in the bay are migratory. Migratory birds travel to find food. They spend only a short time in the bay. Other birds live there year-round. **Waterfowl** are common birds. Herons, egrets, and ibises can be found all across Galveston Bay.

Egrets live for about 15 years in the wild.

*Catfish eat by skimming their mouths along the bottom of the water.

Many finfish live in the bay. Finfish are fish with bones instead of shells. Anchovies are common in the bay. Sea trout and catfish are also common. The finfish are important for birds to eat. There are over 100 species of finfish in Galveston Bay. Like birds, the population has been the same since 2003.

CHAPTER 4

Impact on Plants from Estuaries and Tributaries

Today many kinds of plants and animals can affect the bay. Some of these species are known as **invasive species**. An invasive species is any animal or plant that did not **originate** in an area. Invasive species are brought into the bay by people. Sometimes they bring them by mistake. They come in attached to boats from other places in the world. Sometimes people bring the species in on purpose. No matter how they get there, they can be a problem for **native species**.

The Chinese tallow tree was first brought to the United States from China in the 1700s.

Water hyacinth is often planted in gardens because it is beautiful and grows well.

Some invasive species are plants. In Galveston Bay, one common invasive species is Chinese tallow. Chinese tallow is also known as a popcorn tree. It has red and brown leaves. When it grows, it can take over space from other plants. It also grows berries that are **toxic** to people. Another common invasive species is water hyacinth. This is a beautiful plant that causes big problems in the waterways of the bay. It clogs up the water. It also makes shade that hides sunlight from naturally growing plants. Even underwater plants need sunlight to grow. Native plants in Galveston Bay thrive in shallow water because sunlight can reach them. When invasive species create shade, the native plants can no longer grow.

Sometimes invasive species are animals. The armored catfish is one type. This fish is also called the suckermouth catfish. It likes to burrow into the sand. This makes sandy shores unstable. Unstable shores make it hard for plants to grow. Native plants need shoreline for their roots. The armored catfish also has no natural predators. Its numbers can grow very quickly.

In South America, many people eat armored catfish, although it is not often consumed in the United States.

Zebra mussels also grow quickly. This makes them hard to eliminate. They also take up space native plants need before they get a chance to grow. Zebra mussels are present in the bay. No one knows exactly how they reached the bay. They attach to boats and are easy to spread.

People want to keep the bay healthy. Invasive species threaten the ecosystem. People rely on a healthy bay. Fish need healthy plants to eat. People enjoy eating fish. Without a healthy ecosystem, nothing in the bay can thrive.

* Zebra mussels are named for the stripes on their shells that resemble zebra stripes.

Zebra mussels can survive for 3 to 5 days outside of the water.

CHAPTER 5

Humans and the Bay

The first people to live near the bay were Native Americans. Many tribes lived in the area before the 1700s. People may have lived there up to 14,000 years ago. They fished in the bay. Many of the tribes were **nomadic**. They visited the bay for short time periods. They also relied on rivers for freshwater.

During the late 1700s and 1800s, European immigrants arrived in the area. The new arrivals used the bay for transportation, shipping, and fishing. The first immigrants were from Spain and France. The first map of Galveston Bay was made by a French explorer in 1721. From the beginning, people who lived on the bay had to deal with hurricanes. In 1818, a hurricane destroyed an early settlement.

About 50,000 people live in the city of Galveston, Texas.

Oil from an oil spill can kill fish and other wildlife when it coats their food supply. Oil can also stick to birds' feathers, making it difficult for birds to fly.

During the 1900s, the bay became polluted. Shipping oil leaked into the water. People did not know how much they could change the bay. In the 1900s, people also began drilling for oil in Texas. This created pollution that got into the water.

The bay was also changed because of shipping. People wanted wide ships to be able to pass through the bay. They needed to make the shipping channel larger. From the 1930s through the 1950s, people **dredged** the channel. It grew to be 36 feet (11 m) deep. Today it is even deeper. The Houston Ship Channel is now 42 feet (13 m) deep and 52 miles (84 km) long. This allows very big ships to travel through Galveston Bay.

The 1950s was also when people first began to worry about the water in the bay. The National Environmental Policy Act of 1969 helped protect the bay. It helped create guidelines for how the bay was used. People created groups to protect the bay. The Galveston Bay Foundation was created in 1987. This group works to clean up the bay. The government also works to protect the bay. The Texas legislature recently approved $6.5 million to fight against invasive species. This will help fight for cleaner water throughout the state, including Galveston Bay.

* Since 1986, 533,000 volunteers have helped clean up garbage through the Galveston Bay Adopt-a-Beach Program.

Supertankers are the largest oil tankers in the world. A supertanker can hold up to 2 million barrels of oil.

Galveston Bay is affected by the people that live nearby. Pollution is created by chemicals people use. This pollution can make it difficult for plants to grow. The bay can also affect the people in cities like Galveston and Houston. If the water is unsafe to drink, people will get sick. People can also be harmed by eating seafood from the bay that is contaminated. All of the changes in Galveston Bay are called coastal change. These changes include sea level rise and changing temperatures caused by climate change.

What Can YOU Do for the Bay?

One of the biggest threats to Galveston Bay is trash, which makes its way from the city into the bay's waters. People who want to help keep the bay clean can start by reducing their waste. Start by replacing single-use items such as straws, plastic water bottles, and plastic storage bags with reusable items. Cleaning up trash on streets, in parks, and around the water is another  way to help. For larger amounts of pollution, or trash that can't be reached easily, local families can download the free Galveston Bay Action Network app. The app allows users to take pictures of trash and pollution with their phones. The pictures are sent to groups who are equipped to handle larger cleanups. These small efforts can help keep Galveston Bay clean for years to come.

★ Two feet of rain fell in the first 24 hours of Hurricane Harvey, causing massive flooding.

Coastal change in Galveston Bay means that people, animals, and plants have to adapt. Human beings are better at adapting than animals and plants. Galveston Bay might see bigger changes in the future. Warmer water due to climate change could mean more hurricanes. In 2017, Hurricane Harvey hit Galveston Bay and the surrounding areas. It was one of the worst hurricanes in American history. The future of Galveston Bay will include protecting wildlife as well as protecting people from dangerous changes.

ACTIVITY

Hurricane in a Bowl

Materials:

* Large clear bowl
* Water
* Food coloring (two colors)
* Spoon or stick for stirring
* Notebook and pen for notes

Steps:

1 Find a partner to make a hurricane with! Gather your supplies and take them carefully to a workspace.

2 Decide who will be making the first hurricane and who will be recording. Later on, you will trade places.

3 Fill your bowl almost to the top with clean water.

4 One person will create a hurricane by placing a drop of food coloring into the water.

5 Using a spoon or stick, slowly swirl the water in one direction. This is like hurricane winds moving through the air and water.

6 The other partner should be recording what they see. Think about the questions below.

7 Once you have finished stirring, wait until the water stops moving. Keep taking notes.

8 Repeat steps three through seven after you have traded places.

9 Compare notes and discuss the answers to the questions below.

Questions:

* How does the food coloring move through the water?

* Can you see any shapes in the colors?

* How does it change as you keep stirring?

* How does it change as you stop stirring?

* How do you think this is like a hurricane?

* How do you think this would affect the water in a bay like Galveston Bay?

Glossary

atmosphere *(AT-muhs-feer)* part of the planet made of air

biosphere *(BYE-oh-sfeer)* part of the planet made of living things

converting *(kun-VUR-ting)* changing one thing into another

dredged *(DREJD)* deepened a body of water by removing mud, sand, or other substances

ecosystem *(EE-koh-sis-tum)* the system made up of all the parts of an environment

estuary *(EHS-choo-air-ee)* area where a river or tributary meets the ocean

geosphere *(JEE-oh-sfeer)* part of the planet made of solid ground

habitats *(HAB-ih-tats)* natural environments where plants and animals live

humid *(HYOO-mid)* moisture or dampness in the air

hurricanes *(HUR-ih-kayns)* powerful storms with strong winds at sea

hydrosphere *(HYE-droh-sfeer)* part of the planet made of water

invasive species *(in-VAY-siv SPEE-sheez)* plants or animals that are not native to an area and cause harm to other species in that area

native species *(NAY-tiv SPEE-sheez)* plants or animals that naturally live in a location or type of habitat

nomadic *(noh-MAD-ihk)* something that moves from place to place without a single home

originate *(oh-RIH-jih-nayt)* to begin or come into existence

pollution *(puh-LOO-shin)* when the air, land, or water is dirtied by chemicals, waste, or other harmful things

restore *(ree-STOHR)* to return something to its original state

toxic *(TAHX-ihk)* dangerous or containing dangerous elements

tributaries *(TRIH-byu-tair-eez)* smaller rivers or streams that flow into larger rivers or lakes

waterfowl *(WAH-tur-fowl)* birds that live in or around water

For More Information

Books

Felix, Rebecca. *Hurricane Harvey: Disaster in Texas and Beyond.* Minneapolis, MN: Millbrook, 2018.

French, Jess. *What a Waste: Trash, Recycling, and Protecting Our Planet.* New York, NY: DK Publishing, 2019.

Mattern, Joanne. *The Science of Hurricanes.* New York, NY: Cavendish Square, 2019.

Websites

National Geographic Kids Save the Ocean
https://www.natgeokids.com/uk/discover/animals/sea-life/marine-wildlife-protection
You can read about actions you can take to help save marine life.

Galveston Bay Facts
https://kids.kiddle.co/Galveston_Bay
Learn many new facts about Galveston Bay.

Science Kids Hurricane Facts
http://www.sciencekids.co.nz/sciencefacts/weather/hurricane.html
Are you interested in how hurricanes work? You can find out more here.

Index

armored catfish, 20

Chinese tallow, 18, 19
Christmas Bay Coastal Preserve, 11

East Bay, 6, 9
Environmental Policy Act of 1969, 24

finfish, 17

Gulf of Mexico, 4, 5, 6

Houston, Texas, 4, 5, 7, 9, 24, 26
humans, 10, 11, 14

Hurricane Harvey, 27

oysters, 10, 11, 12, 15

San Jacinto River, 5, 8
sea grass, 10, 12, 14
shrimp, 13

toxins, 5
Trinity River, 5, 8

watershed, 8, 10, 11
West Bay, 6, 9

About the Author

M. Weber loves to write for kids. She has written about cities, animals, and the world around us. She lives in Minnesota with her husband and son.